RIDING for Everybody

The noble beast

RIDING

Peter

LONDON

for Everybody

Churchill

BLANDFORD PRESS

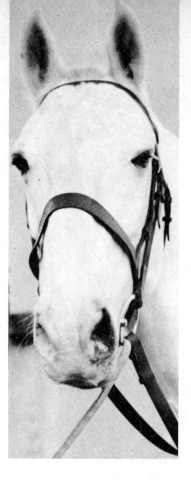

DEDICATION
To Topper—a far better instructor than I

First published 1962
Second edition 1966
Third edition 1969

© *Blandford Press Ltd, 1962*
167 High Holborn, London, WC1

Printed in Great Britain by
Jarrold and Sons Ltd, Norwich

Contents

Page

1 A General Introduction   7

2 Learning to Ride   12
CHOOSING A RIDING SCHOOL
NOTES ON DRESS FOR THE BEGINNER

3 A History of Equitation
and Horsemastership   19

4 The Equipment of Horse and Rider   24

5 Equitation   36

6 Jumping   53

7 Riding Manners   58

8 Riding Activities   63

9 Buying Your Own Horse   70
SOME EQUESTRIAN TERMINOLOGY   75
ACKNOWLEDGMENTS   80

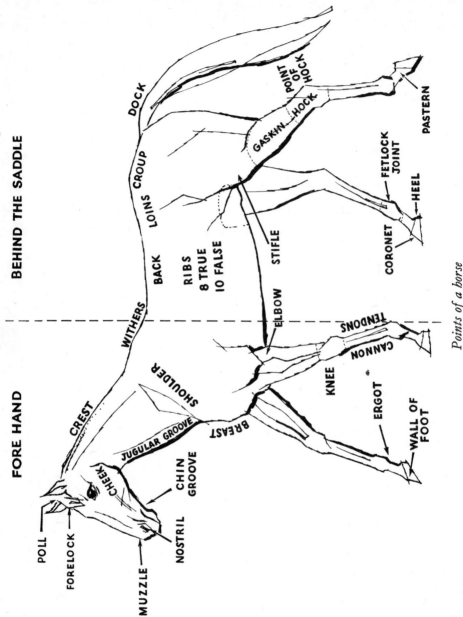

Points of a horse

1 A General Introduction

IN RECENT YEARS riding has become a sport for everybody, and is no longer a sport for the wealthy few or a profession into which retired Army officers disappear. There are many reasons for this modern interest in the horse. One of the strongest is the advent of television, a medium which has shown millions of families the thrills and beauty of the large international horse shows and horse trials. Gradually people began to realise, particularly the younger ones, that here was a sport which they could enjoy all the year round.

For riding is one of the most accommodating of sports. It is a pastime that the whole family can enjoy; you are never too old to learn to ride, at least well enough to be able to enjoy yourself thoroughly. It is a hobby that one can follow both winter and summer, for the horse is never out of season. As a physical exercise it is very good for spastic children, and certain cases of polio and tuberculosis. It is a good healthy outdoor sport. As a mental exercise, I can thoroughly recommend it for harassed housewives, hectic businessmen, and spoilt children! So the horse, although a luxury in some ways, has a new and useful part to play in the community.

Learning to ride should be a slow and carefully planned process, studying first the horse as a living personality, which he indeed is, and then training oneself into the correct mental attitude towards the horse and riding as an art, which is needed if one wishes to ride well. At first it will be uncomfortable, and perhaps nerve racking, but once achieved you will obtain the golden key to a world of joy, thrills, and the sense of satisfaction that only this wonderful creature can give you. I hasten to add that along with the joy and the thrills will also come some disappointments and heartaches, but these, I feel, will always be a normal part of life anyway.

People are beginning to appreciate real equitation. Not so long ago, on pulling into one's local garage, the main topic of conversation would be horse-racing or greyhounds. People knew all the top jockeys and trainers, their favourite racecourses and the rules of the Jockey Club. Now they know the show jumpers, their riders, the rules of the British Show Jumping Association, and they appreciate such finer arts as horse trials and dressage. Not that I am inferring that jockeys are not equestrians, for I know that some of them are very competent horsemen.

To my mind this trend towards the horse and riding is a very good thing. The horse has been rapidly disappearing from our industrial and agricultural scene, and employment for him was becoming very scarce, but now we have this expanding new body of riders, those who might be called "casual" or "weekend" riders, to offer more security to the future of this noble beast.

I feel it is now that we, who like to think we are "horsey", should enlighten as many people as possible on the care of the horse and riding, and encourage as many people as possible to ride correctly, using definite techniques. Then this enthusiasm for riding can be handed down to future generations and the new-found employment for horses will continue indefinitely.

One of the first steps in learning to ride is to gain as much knowledge and experience as you can of the horse, his personality and his physical characteristics.

At the beginning of the horse's evolution he was a small hunted animal. We know he was originally a hunted creature by the fact that his eyes are set to the side of his head, whereas all hunters, such as ourselves, have their eyes at the front. It seems ironic that Man has now turned him into a hunter. It is because of this natural feeling of being the hunted that the horse by nature is timid, and at some times very nervous. The horse is not an attacking animal; he has no horns, no sharp teeth, no fangs, and no claws. His only method of defence is to run away, and he has natural speed. The horse is not an intelligent animal—I do not mean this in detriment to the horse— and his mental powers have a childlike quality. His brain is extremely sensitive but really quite simple.

Horse showing his objection
(*This has been specially posed*)

The horse has two important mental characteristics which we use in riding him and in training him, and they are, his wonderful memory—easily as good as, if not better than, the elephant's—and his natural generous nature. Do not conclude from this that the horse is servile, because he is not. In fact one can often see, in the show ring or in the local park, horses and ponies —particularly ponies—lodging their objection or refusing to obey their riders' wishes. In the majority of cases the rider is completely oblivious of the fact that the horse is objecting and seems to think that he is playing up! Because of his childlike mentality the horse thrives on routine, which forms the basis of all good training programmes and stable management.

Having established something about the horse's personality, the next step is your own personality, or, more accurately, your mental attitude to riding and the horse. Most learners are nervous or, if not nervous, certainly cautious, when first starting to ride. This is a perfectly natural feeling for both children and adults, and your instructor should allow for this in the preliminary lessons. I would far rather teach a beginner who is nervous, at first, than the bravado of one who appears to think that the horse is just a vehicle to go fast on. It has been proved to me time and time again that the naturally nervous, as distinct from frightened, learner usually makes the most sensitive rider, and what is more important the most considerate. One must always remember that the horse is a living creature, just as you and I, with the same emotions, feelings and fears as we have.

9

One must adopt a definite mental attitude: the horse, again because of his childlike qualities, has no time for indecision. At all times you must try to be definite in your orders or signals. The horse is an animal that is easily confused, and once confused quite unresponsive. So the golden rules should be to decide what you are going to do, how you are going to do it, and when you are going to do it, and to get the message over to the horse clearly and concisely.

Personally, I am not very keen on such terms as "mastering the horse" or "breaking the horse in", because, as I have stated earlier, I consider the horse to be a noble creature and not a servile one. I would rather hear such terms as—"gaining the horse's confidence" and "co-operation". The animal should never be frightened of you nor you of him, and to perform well you must become a team. You will never become a happy team if your horse is your frightened slave. The horse, like us, must of course be corrected if he does wrong, but never forget that the difference between punishment and cruelty is equivalent to the width of a human hair. The punishment must never be greater than the seriousness of the crime. There is only one place to hit a horse, the part where most of the flesh is—the bottom!

On approaching a horse, either in the stable or when mounting, always forewarn him of your coming. Do not dash up to him and say "Hello, darling" (the writer has known this to happen, with serious consequences for the "dasher"!). Walk towards him, slowly but definitely, from the front; let him know you are coming by speaking to him. There is no reason why you should not call him "darling" if you wish to; he will not be embarrassed. Your voice is one of the most important methods of communication you have with your horse, so use it liberally. Do not stretch out your hand unless it contains a tit-bit. When coming alongside him just run your hand down the side of his neck, speak to him again and give him a gentle pat. Remembering at all times that the horse is a naturally timid animal, never wave your hands, legs, arms, or hat about whilst near him. Avoid all movements or noise that may alert him or frighten him.

Never approach a horse from the rear, or any position from which he cannot see you. And never approach him from any position that may make your appearance startle him. It is only his natural timidity

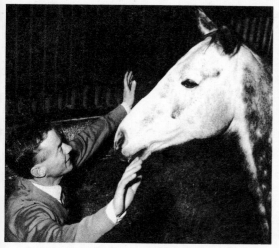 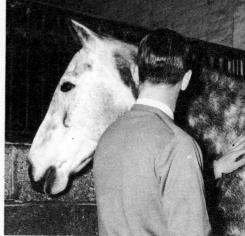

The wrong way to approach a horse in his box (Luckily Scampi knows me!)

The correct way to approach a horse in his box

that makes the horse "lash out" with his hind legs, never the desire to do you harm. Your sudden appearance, without forewarning, may frighten him.

All good and respected horsemen and stablemen when in the stable are quiet of voice and gentle of movement. Do not accept the popular belief, in fact legend, that horsey people are loud of mouth; they are certainly not. If you ever walk into a stable yard where the staff and instructors—and female ones are particularly prone to this—are loud-mouthed, then do not accept these pseudo people as horsey experts. So many of these "Walter Mitty" instructors and instructresses seem to think that being a riding instructor is the same as being a regimental sergeant-major. Nothing is further from the truth.

With horses we are always learning, and if we lived to be a hundred we would never know everything. Nothing gives the half-knowledge horseman away more than his belief that he knows it all, as this is an impossibility.

Aim at perfection; you will never reach it, but it is well worth trying to get as near as possible to it.

2 Learning to Ride

HAVING FIRST DECIDED that you really do want to learn to ride, your second step is where to ride—choosing your riding school. This stage is just as important as your preliminary lessons; you must be fully confident that you are going to get good instruction, and to benefit from the instruction you must have complete confidence and respect for your riding instructor, his knowledge and his horses. The riding school business is one of those rare professions, I am sorry to say, into which almost anyone can enter. There is no legislation to say what type of person, or what type of qualifications, a riding school proprietor must be or must have. Therefore the choosing of a riding school to the uninitiated can be a problem. I have people coming to me practically every week who say that they have been riding for two or three years, and when I get them mounted I find that they have not the slightest idea of the simple basic principles of equitation. On investigating further, I usually find that they have spent two years "being a passenger" on some poor unfortunate creature just capable of carrying them over the downs or around the park for an hour. The sorry thing is that they, the riders, have been given the impression that learning to ride is sitting on the horse as often as possible. So for the sake of the horse, for the sake of riding and for the sake of the future, one must be "choosey" in choosing a riding school. It is with this in mind that I have written this chapter.

A riding school is really no different from your hairdresser or your tailor, the fundamental objective should be the same, to give value for money and good service. You would not patronise a hairdresser long if he did not do your hair to your satisfaction, and you would not visit the same tailor twice, if the suit he made for you was not a good fit. As with so many things in life, it is not always the cheapest which is the best. There is no such thing as "cheap" riding lessons, because there is no such thing as a cheap way of keeping horses, certainly not horses which are in first-rate condition as those in a riding school need to be.

At one local show I remember speaking to what an outsider would assume to be an experienced horseman. The topic of conversation was one of my favourites—that of riding schools, of course. This fellow, who has never owned a riding school, thank goodness, announced that it was impossible to make a riding school really pay. My ears immediately "cocked" at hearing this, as I make a comfortable living out of mine, and have done so for some time. He then went on to say that a profit margin could only be made by cutting feeding costs. This, at first, made me red with anger, but on thinking it over I have realised that this way of thinking must form the basis of the costing systems of many riding schools: that is not to cost a profit margin but to cut costs to make one. This, I consider, is where many riding schools are failing. Running a successful riding school is the same as running an engineering firm or a button factory, in that it is essential for it to have a sound costing and business foundation. These points must be borne in mind when choosing a riding school.

The first step is to find out the names of the riding schools in your area, and establish where they are. This you can do with the help of the British Horse Society, the official body of the horsey world. They will give you the names, addresses and telephone numbers of the schools within your area. The British Horse Society will also inform you as to whether the schools they have mentioned have been approved by them. Their inspectors, when invited, inspect and issue a badge of approval, if they are satisfied with the establishment. The operative phrase here is "when invited", as the Society will only inspect a riding school at the invitation of the proprietors. If the inspectors are satisfied that the establishment is well managed, that the horses are properly kept and of the right type, and that the instructors do actually teach, then they will issue the school with a badge of approval. If your local school holds this badge then you have very little to worry about. If however it does not, this does not necessarily mean that it is a bogus school.

Well, what other methods can you use to choose your school? There are two: (1) Ask your local veterinary surgeon's advice; (2) Go to a school and assess it for yourself. I suggest you do both of these things. All riding schools are supposed to be inspected, periodically, by a veterinary surgeon appointed by the local council. The inspection is aimed purely at the soundness of the horses and ponies. Veterinary surgeons, that is horsey ones, I have found to be very shrewd men; they see more than one would think and they hear more than one would think. So who better to give you advice on the local riding schools than the local veterinary surgeon? Go and see him, even if he charges you for it. His information will be worth having.

The second method is to go along and have a look at the place yourself. First let us analyse the impression the place should give you, and then the impression the place should not give you. You do not have to know anything about horses to make your assessment; remember you are a prospective customer and you want good service. It is better to telephone first and make an appointment, rather than just turn up. If the school is busy, there will not be much time to spend talking to you and you may be in the way.

The stables should be clean, well laid out and airy. Obviously, if the staff are in the middle of putting bedding down or mucking out the horses, the place will be rather untidy, but nevertheless one should be able to judge the cleanliness of the stables. There should be an air of organisation and the staff should be quietly spoken around the horses and the stableyard. The proprietor, or his representative,

One cannot expect all stables to look like this; good premises are difficult to find: but they can still be well laid out and organised

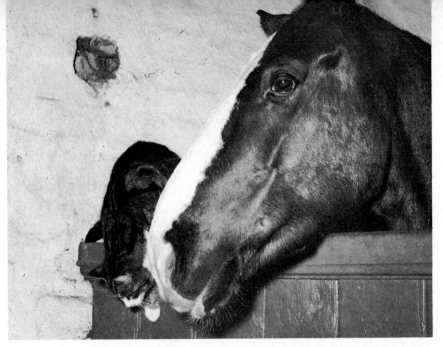

Kismet and Cumgee. Note the bright, interested look in Kismet's eye

should be at least twenty-five years old. I do not feel that anyone younger than this could have sufficient *professional* experience, and I do stress the word professional, to own or manage a really efficient riding school. He should be smart and clean in appearance. This does not mean that he should be dressed in the very smartest and expensive riding wear; if he were then he might not be a very practical horseman. There is no room for glamour in professional riding instruction. What I do mean, though, is that if the proprietor greets you collarless and showing his braces, then make a quick exit. If he greets a new client this way, what will happen once you become a client?

There is no need for you to know anything about horses to make a simple evaluation of the mounts available at the school, or of their welfare. If you weigh fourteen stone, and there is no reason why a person weighing fourteen stone should not learn to ride, then have a look and see that there are some big horses available, at least one; if not then make a quick exit again. I should mention here that on your first visit the Principal should take you on a conducted tour of the stables and his animals. You can judge the horses yourself by observing two points. First the eyes. Horses have very expressive eyes and they should be bright and alive and have that "interested in life" look, which, in fact, all healthy living things should have. The second is the horse's coat. This should look clean and well kept and, like the eyes, should be bright. It should be rather silky to the touch. This is all you need know at this stage to give you a guide to a healthy and happy horse.

Remember that the Principal whom you are judging is going to be responsible for you, for children, perhaps your children, and for your future enjoyment of this wonderful pastime, riding

Now for the impression that the school should *not* give you. It should not be untidy and messy, there should be no nasty smell—the smell of horses, unless your nose is very sensitive, should not be obnoxious, it should be a rather pleasant "country" type of smell. There should not be dozens of young children running wild around the place. You will always find dozens of children around a stable, but they should be well behaved. The stables should not be dark with a damp and musty feel about them; the horses should not be scruffy or dejected looking. The Principal should not be a gruff, rough and ready type, and certainly not a teenager!

Having made your decision and chosen your riding school, you are now ready to learn to ride. There must be many questions you ask yourself here, particularly if you are an adult learner, such as; "Am I going to make a fool of myself?" "Will I fall off and get hurt?" "What is going to happen to me?" "Will I be stiff?" and "What am I going to wear?"

To take the last question first: for your first few lessons there is no need for you to wear the complete riding kit, so do not go rushing off to spend all your hard-earned money on buying the entire uniform. I do advise, though, that right from the very beginning you wear a hard riding hat. This is not very expensive and it will be money well spent. The hats are smart-looking, sensible, and a very important safety factor. There is no sense in spending a lot of money on the correct clothes, at this stage. Find out first whether you are going to like riding, whether you are going to progress at it, and whether you are going to like horses.

It is advisable to have a fairly close-fitting pair of slacks or trousers, a thick sweater or jacket, and a pair of walking shoes or if possible a pair of jodhpur boots. By walking shoes, I mean a pair of shoes with a low and well defined heel, with emphasis on "low". I have known female riders to turn up for their first lesson wearing high heels which could, besides being a hindrance, be very dangerous whilst learning to ride.

As you progress with your riding, so you can progress with your riding dress.

"Am I going to make a fool of myself?" I know many adults who have asked themselves this question, and the simple answer is, "Of course you are not". When learning anything new, one is going to make mistakes, obvious ones, silly ones, big ones and small ones—we all do. A well-trained instructor, whether he is teaching riding or bridge, should expect you to make these mistakes and help you to solve them. We all make mistakes and feel fools when we start, but nobody will laugh at you. They might laugh with you, when you first start riding, because we all had to start at the beginning just as you are doing.

It is only natural that after the first one or two lessons you are going to be stiff, particularly your upper thigh muscles, as these are rarely used in other sports. The old story of not being able to sit down

The leading rein

for a week after your first lesson is not a very accurate one. Riding and ski-ing are, I believe, two of the few sports that ask you to co-ordinate every muscle in your body and your mental powers at the same time. So do not worry if you are stiff at first, your muscles will soon become attuned to the exercise and the stiffness will get less and less after each lesson.

Your first lessons should be gentle and slow, being introduced to the horse, getting the feel of his movement underneath you and suppling up your muscles. Your preliminary lessons will be on a leading rein, that is being led from the instructor's horse, or on a lungeing rein in a paddock or indoor arena. The lungeing rein is a long webbing rein, approximately 25 to 30 ft, which allows the instructor to stand whilst you and your mount walk around him. At about the second or third lesson your instructor should outline to you his general plan for the remainder of your preliminary lessons. At this stage he should have made a general assessment of you, how much you should do, how quickly or slowly he feels you will progress, and from what he has seen of your nature and your personality how you are going to take to riding. All good teaching must have a sound basic formula.

There is such a thing as a natural rider. And there is such a thing as an "inborn" rider. But it is my firm belief that practically anybody can be taught to ride well enough to enjoy themselves thoroughly, and with a high degree of enjoyment and comfort to the horse.

Never, never be in a hurry when learning to ride—don't try to gallop before you can walk!

The lungeing rein

3   A History of Equitation and Horsemastership

THE HORSE WAS ORIGINALLY A SMALL ANIMAL, about the size of a fox. He was a grazing animal and a hunted animal. Nature soon provided him with longer legs so that he might escape his enemies, and somewhere along the line Man began to train him. Man's two main reasons for training the horse were (*a*) as a means of conveyance, and (*b*) as a vehicle of war. From these beginnings stemmed equitation.

A man's skill with sword, lance, and horse has been from the earliest times the success by which his stature as a gentleman has been measured. Every nobleman had horses and practically every nobleman had his own private riding school and riding instructor.

In all the Royal Courts, right back to the beginning of royalty, a riding school could be found. The Royal riding instructor was an important and respected member of the Royal Household, who was responsible for the working horses, the war horses and the riding horses, and for entertaining the members of the Court with high school displays. It was he who influenced and, in many ways, altered the way of thinking with regard to horses and riding prevailing at

19

Horsemen in the Panathenaic Procession. About 440 B.C. Notice the riders' positions, particularly their hands and the deepness of their seats, and compare with the riders of today.

his particular time in history. So we find that the great art of equitation has risen or declined with the social conditions and fashions of each era.

Most of the dressage and high school movements we use today have an extremely long history, being based originally upon battle movements and displays designed to entertain royalty.

Many of the methods we use today to ride and train the horse derived from the experience and teachings of two great horsemen, Kikkulis and Xenophon. Kikkulis was horsemaster to the kings of the Hittites, in the country of Mitanni, the famous Hittite horsemen. His instructions on horsemastership and equitation were recorded in 1400 B.C. on five tablets, which were found in the archives of the kings of the Hittites.

His methods must have been gained from experience, so I think it is safe to say that there had, most probably, been many serious horsemasters before. It is interesting to note that the teaching of Kikkulis was that the horse should be trained by kindness, so gaining the confidence and co-operation of the animal. He never advocated force.

Xenophon wrote the next important work on horses and riding, in 400 B.C. Here again was a man who used kindness and co-operation, and many of his methods of stable management and the keeping of the fit horse would satisfy most modern trainers.

It was these two early horsemasters who first said that the horse could be trained up to a higher state of fitness by being kept in a stable, and that the horse kept outside would develop what they called a "hay belly", but what we call a "grass tummy". They claimed that the horse carrying a "hay belly" would never withstand really hard galloping, and this is still absolutely true today. As the horses at that time were required to gallop very long distances pulling chariots, these men obviously knew their jobs.

With the arrival of the Roman Empire, equitation, like so many arts began to decline. It was nearly two thousand years before anything outstanding was written on the subject.

This came in 1569 with the teachings of Frederico Grisone. Grisone advocated sheer brute force as the method by which the horse should be trained. The horse was now becoming, not only an instrument of battle, but also a fashionable medium of entertainment. In order to get the horse to perform complicated and intricate steps, Grisone used cruelty, and many of the horses at that time were completely muscle-bound because of the restrictive and demanding training programme they were put through. The horse was the complete slave of his master. Other writers advocated the same brutal methods, including Pignatelli in 1612 and the Duke of Newcastle in his book *The Art of Horseman-ship* in 1657.

In 1666 a book, *L'Instruction du Roi!* was written by Antoine de Pluvinel, in the form of a conversation with Louis XIII, to whom he was riding instructor. Pluvinel's techniques were based on the two original principles of kindness, and gaining the horse's confidence and co-operation. This was frowned upon, and it was thanks largely to Louis XIII that his methods left their mark upon equitation.

The Arabian conquest of Spain had a tremendous influence on Spanish equitation and methods of training, the Arabs being particularly intelligent horsemen, and perhaps the first race of people to give any serious thought to the breeding of fine horses. It was three Arab stallions, brought to this country, that formed the basis of the thoroughbred as we know him today. Their names were: the Godolphin Arabian, the Darley Arabian, and the Byerley Turk.

It was through M. de la Gueriniere's teachings and methods that equitation and horsemastership reached its peak. He was the first man to state that all horses, whatever their future uses, should receive early basic training in obedience and flexibility. This was the forerunner of what we now call dressage. He also had as the basis of his teaching, kindness and co-operation as the right methods in training.

During the French Revolution there was a sharp decline in England and in France in the art of riding and training the horse. This art was replaced by the less exacting training of the heavy horse for war.

In 1918 Max Von Weyrother was appointed manager of the Spanish Riding School of Vienna, and it was during this year that equitation and horsemastership reached its former peak. This school which breeds and uses Lippizan stallions is still the finest riding academy in the world. The riders are trained to ride in what is known as the classical or academic style. It is interesting to note that, although the style and method of schooling is still based upon the teachings of Von Weyrother, the riders sit into the middle of their saddles and their mounts, this being one of the basic fundamentals of the seat now used.

With the birth of the twentieth century has come a crop of horsemasters and equestrians, perhaps never equalled before in the history of the art. When I mention horsemasters and horsemen, I also include horsemistresses (if there is such a word), and horsewomen, as there has been quite a number of brilliant women exponents of the art.

Modern man has adapted modern thinking to equitation. Modern science has improved horsemastership and veterinary techniques beyond any of the wildest hopes Kikkulis could have thought possible. Feeding the horse, always a great art, has become a science, too, and the horse has benefited tremendously from new medicines and drugs.

It is interesting to note one very major change that has taken place in the technique of riding. There were two men largely responsible for this, an Italian named Capprilli and an American, Tod Sloan.

Tod Sloan was a jockey. It is claimed he was the first race rider to adopt the technique of using shorter stirrup leathers and the position of a crouch behind the racehorse's neck, a style popularly known in America as the "monkey seat". Sloan came to this country to demonstrate the new style. At first it received a great deal of criticism from the die-hard English racing folk, but they soon realised the sound common sense behind the revolutionary method. It was Sloan's theory that with a shorter leather and the low crouching position, the jockey was able to keep his body weight in better relation to the racehorse's centre of gravity, the centre of gravity being approximately below the saddle girth. It was also thought, and later proved, that by crouching down low behind the racehorse's neck, the jockey could cut down the wind-resistance when travelling fast, thus enabling the horse to travel much faster.

Tod Sloan had tremendous success with this method, proving it to be better by far than the old. This style is now generally adopted (and generally abused, in my opinion), throughout the world.

Caprilli was one of the founders, or certainly the architect, of a style of riding known as the forward impulse. He shocked the horsey world in the early 1900s, by riding with a much shorter stirrup and

positioning himself in a more forward position. Added to this, he rode with a shorter but freer rein, allowing the horse more freedom with his neck. One can draw a definite parallel between the techniques of Tod Sloan and Caprilli, although they were from two distinct worlds, in so much as both men wanted to achieve the best results in the way most natural to the horse.

Caprilli devoted his life to perfecting the forward impulse. He spent many hours studying the movements of horses romping about in fields. Many times to his own personal injury, he experimented riding horses over varying types of jumps, at all paces, and cross-country, to evolve his method. The Italian Government (Caprilli was a cavalry officer) recognised his work and gave him every facility and financial help. I do not think the Italians will ever regret it.

The basic fundamental of the forward impulse—and here I think is where one can draw the parallel—is for the rider to sit in such a way that he follows the natural movements of the horse. His teaching quite simply was that: the rider should at all times keep his weight over the horse's centre of gravity, the horse should be given greater freedom to use his neck and his head, his natural balancing pole. This teaching formed the basis of the general-purpose seat which we now use.

Pierro Santini, also an Italian cavalry officer, has written many books on the forward impulse of which he was a great exponent.

The horse has had a long and varying history, and I have tried in these pages to give you a chronological and brief, yet, I hope, understandable outline. I hope that we will never see the return of brutal methods to gain the submission of this noble beast.

4 The Equipment of Horse and Rider

IN THE EARLY STAGES OF YOUR RIDING LIFE—I purposely use the word "life", because if you have been started off correctly you will never want to give it up—you should begin to learn as much as possible about the equipment of the horse and rider, that is, the tools of the trade.

Before going any further may I state here and now that one saddles up a horse or tacks up a horse. One does not dress or undress a horse. Many learners fall into the trap of saying "Shall I dress my horse?" or "undress" him. This will cause a great deal of laughter in the stable. So to save you this embarrassment, remember, we tack up or saddle up our mounts.

Whilst it is not my intention to give you a running commentary on the various and many different types of bits and saddles, I do intend to illustrate to you what I consider to be a well equipped and turned out horse. It would take a volume of books to describe all the shapes, forms and sizes that saddlery has taken through the years, much of which has been invented and designed by Man for Man, and in very few cases by Man for horse, and never by the horse or his Creator for the horse. My one pipedream in life is that one day a horse will design a set of saddlery for Man!

It was Pierro Santini, the famous Italian equestrian, who once said "simplicity is difficult and complication is easy". This should always be the motto of all horsemen and horsewomen when considering the equipment to be worn by the horse, in fact in everything to do with the horse and riding.

Nor do I intend to write reams on the technicalities of bitting or mouthing. Much too much has been written on this subject already, some of which would have been better left unwritten, and some upon which I could never improve. I will deal purely and simply with the action, and the fitting of the bridle and bit, the basic and elementary principles, and what happens when it is in your hands.

24

Here is the horse equipped for competition riding.
Although one cannot generalise on the type of equipment,
the basic formula is more or less the same in all cases

The bit is our means of control and interpretation, and through the reins to the bit we get our "feel" of the horse. The bit should lie upon the bars of the horse's mouth, that is to say, the upper portion of the lower jaw. It is here where the extra sensitive nerves are housed close to the skin. By applying pressure on the bit, we apply pain upon the bars. Thus comes the first basic principle of control. By releasing the pressure on the bit we reward the horse, and so comes the second basic principle of control. Now we can bring control down to its simplest form as—reward and correction—just by knowing two basic facts of the action of the bit. Easy isn't it?

There are two types of bit popularly used in riding schools—the Snaffle bit and the Pelham bit.

The Snaffle is perhaps the simplest form of bit ever designed. As you can see from the illustration, it comprises two rings joined by a bar which is jointed in the middle and which goes into the horse's mouth. The Snaffle is used with only one rein, and is made of nickel, stainless steel, or rubber. The thinner the mouthpiece, then the more severe the action of the bit. This applies to all kinds of bit.

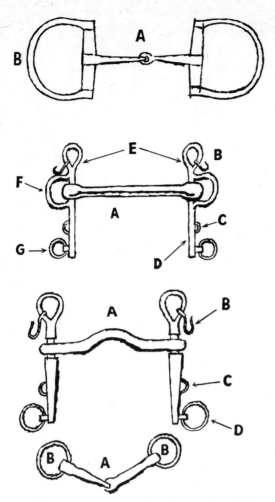

THE D TYPE SNAFFLE
A *Jointed mouthpiece*
B *"D" rings where reins are attached*

THE PELHAM
A *Straight mouthpiece*
B *Upper cheek*
C *Lip strap attaches here*
D *Lower cheek*
E *Hooks for curb chain*
F *Rein attaches here*
G *Curb rein attaches here*

THE DOUBLE BRIDLE
A *Mouthpiece of bit and jointed mouthpiece of bridoon*
B *Hooks for curb chain. Snaffle rein attaches here*
C *Lip strap fittings*
D *Curb rein rings*

Note when fitting, the bridoon should lie above the bit

The best type of Snaffle is the "D" ringed bit. The reason is that because of its physical characteristics there is no likelihood of its being pulled through the sides of the horse's mouth by a beginner or for that matter by an experienced rider.

If you are considering any form of competition work, then the "D" ringed Snaffle is the bit I would recommend. In fact, I would recommend this bit for all forms of riding, providing the horse has a Snaffle mouth. That is to say that he can be controlled correctly and comfortably in a plain Snaffle.

Remember, if you have to decide which bit a horse is to wear, that it is better to "go up the scales" and not work your way down. First try the simplest and mildest form of bit on the horse, then if necessary, and I sincerely hope it never will be, work your way up to the stronger and more severe bits.

For any horse that is bit-shy or bit-conscious, that is, a horse which one finds difficult to educate in accepting the bit, usually because he has an extra sensitive mouth, the soft rubber Snaffle can be a very fine bit. I do emphasise, though, that it must be of soft rubber. I personally see no value, rhyme or reason, in the vulcanite versions of rubber bits. To my mind a bit is made of rubber so that it is flexible and soft—then why vulcanise it? One note of warning here concerning the soft rubber Snaffle. It does have disadvantages. They are its tendency to "burn" the mouth if not applied correctly, and its tendency to be a little "dead" in your hands. I have found the latter is generally caused by the horse being allowed to "lay" or "hang" on it. By these expressions I mean that the horse has been allowed to counteract the control of the hands and the bit by taking the pressure on his lips against the softness and give of the rubber, thus defeating the object of the two basic principles of control—reward and correction.

The Pelham is what I call a half-way bit, that is to say it is neither a Double nor a Snaffle. The double bridle is illustrated with the Pelham. The Pelham is a combination between the two bits used in the double bridle. I believe it was designed originally for the army, so that the troopers (and, I suspect, most officers) could ride their horses with ample control, though lacking in knowledge, and with the minimum discomfort and harm to their mounts. I find the Pelham a very good everyday working bit for riding school use, my reasons being the same as the army's, who are always down to earth and practical!

The basic action of the Pelham is the same as the Snaffle, but with the addition of a curb chain and curb rein. The curb chain is fitted in the chin groove just behind the lower jaw, thus giving greater leverage upon the bars of the mouth and the tongue. Remember that the curb chain is supposed to be painless so make sure that it is. When the curb chain is fitted it should lie flat against the horse's chin groove, loose enough for you to place your hand behind it.

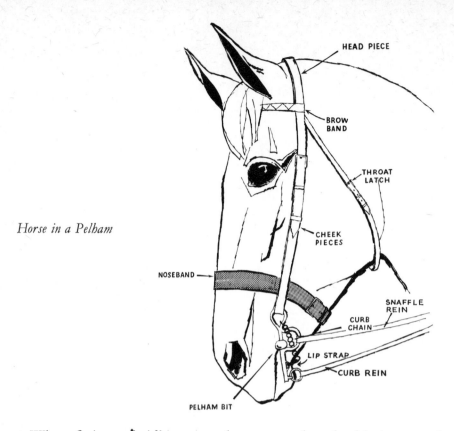

Horse in a Pelham

HEAD PIECE

BROW BAND

THROAT LATCH

CHEEK PIECES

NOSEBAND

SNAFFLE REIN

CURB CHAIN

LIP STRAP

CURB REIN

PELHAM BIT

When fitting a bridle onto a horse, see that the bit is properly adjusted in the mouth. It should not be tight enough to crease the lips, and should not be loose enough to allow the horse to play with the bit with his tongue. The former will cause great discomfort to your mount, and the latter is liable to encourage mouth vices.

The most common mouth vice is when the horse puts his tongue over the bit; once a horse starts this it is extremely difficult to correct. By putting his tongue over the bit the horse evades its action. This will cause him great a deal of unnecessary pain and worry, and the rider will find it difficult to get the horse to go quietly.

Like so many of the aspects of equitation and horsemastership, bitting and mouthing is a science unto itself. So do not dabble in it unless you have been properly trained. I say this not for your sake, but for the sake of the horse, for generally he is the sufferer.

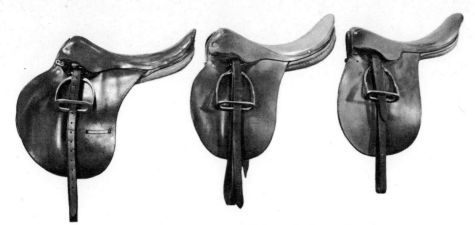

Left to right: A jumping saddle (note the forward cut flap), a general purpose saddle, a straight ordinary saddle

THE SADDLE

I have illustrated three different types of saddle—the straight English saddle, which is as out of date as solid tyres on the motor car, the jumping saddle, and the general purpose saddle. Once again, as with bits, I do not intend writing a Saddler's Sales Catalogue. I am purely describing what I have found through hard experience, the most practical saddle for teaching people to ride in (not *on*—*in!*). The general purpose saddle is the most suitable one for this purpose. It is, as its name implies, a saddle for general purposes. The one I intend dealing with is known as the Kennett, but they are all more or less the same. The saddle is designed to place the rider in the correct and most comfortable position, that is in the middle of the horse, and the lowest part of

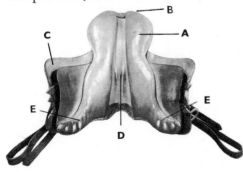

A *The panel of the saddle, which in this case is leather*
B *The cantle*
C *The flaps of the saddle*
D *The channel or gullet*
E *The knee rolls*

29

the saddle. Thus the back of the saddle is higher and the upward curve more acute, giving a deep, secure, and comfortable seat. The more comfort you get from your saddle, then the more sensitive your seat will become. By seat, I mean your position in the saddle, and not any specific part of your anatomy. The Kennett is fitted with knee rolls, giving support to the upper thighs and allowing the leg to hang in the correct position. The panel and saddle flaps are designed to allow the maximum use of the legs, and so that you can feel your mount underneath you. Remember, "feel" is the very basis of the "telephone system" between you and your mount.

SADDLE CLOTHS

I always use a saddle cloth, either of the woollen or linen variety, simply because I believe that, no matter how perfectly my saddle fits my horse, it is good to have something of a soft nature between skin and leather, particularly if the horse is going to be schooled or worked every day. Saddle pads should not be necessary if the saddle is fitted correctly, but there are times when one has to use them and they should always be of the soft variety.

The bell shape stirrup iron

EYE FOR
STIRRUP LEATHER

THE STIRRUP IRONS

The stirrup irons should be of the bell shape variety, as illustrated. The heavier the iron the better, within reason of course. Practically every horseman's Number One dread is to be caught up in the stirrup iron, in a fall, and be dragged by his mount. Providing that the foot can slip comfortably in and out of the iron, that the iron is heavy enough to remain in its correct position whilst empty, and that the iron is of the correct height to allow the foot to be released from it at an upward or downward angle, then the chances of the rider getting hung up should be remote. Note here that too big an iron is just as dangerous as too small an iron. When the horse is standing unmounted the iron should hang naturally on the stirrup leather at right angles to the ground. The stirrup leather should fit snuggly into the eye at the top of the iron, so counteracting any movement between the leather and iron whilst you are performing.

GIRTHS

There are many types of girth made from leather, webbing, nylon string, and for racing one can even get an elastic girth that breathes with the horse. It does not really matter which type of girth you ride with, providing two simple points have been observed. These are that the girth is thoroughly and regularly cleaned (and that does not mean being made just to look nice) and that it is checked regularly to see that it is not pinching or chafing the horse. Regular cleaning, of course, applies to all saddlery and equipment allied to the horse and riding.

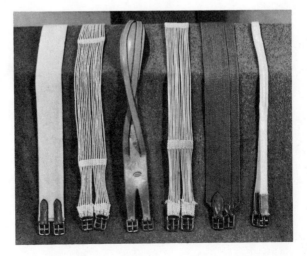

Six types of girth, all well tried and found to be successful

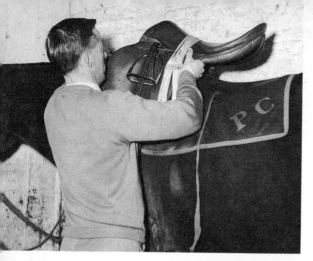

The first stage in putting on the saddle

The second stage in putting on the saddle

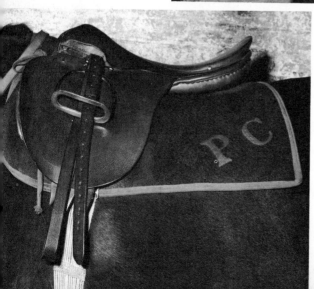

Here is the saddle fitted. Note that the girth is well clear of the horse's elbow, so that the chances of chafing are cut down to a minimum

PUTTING ON THE SADDLE

Place your saddle cloth into position, being very careful to see that all the horse's hairs are lying the correct way. Before placing the saddle into position, see that the stirrup irons are at the top of the leathers and that the girth is folded neatly over the waist of the saddle. Standing on the left hand (near) side of the horse, slide the saddle, moving away from his head towards his tail, into position. The pommel should fit snuggly over the withers, and you should be able to put your hand between the pommel and the horse's withers. The back of the saddle should clear his spine. Check that the saddle cloth has not moved and is lying flat. Then move to the right hand (off) side, bring the girth over *gently*, check that it is not twisted. Now move back to the near side, bring the girth under the horse, buckle it up to finger pressure only at first, then check that you have placed it clear of his elbows. Finally, as with the bridle, check the complete thing again.

PUTTING ON THE BRIDLE

First take the bridle in your left hand, then with your right hand *gently* place the reins over the horse's neck. Pass the top part of the bridle into your right hand, stand with right cheek to the horse's left

Stages in putting on the bridle. The second photo shows the correct amount of tightness needed in the throat latch and noseband. Notice the bit hangs quite comfortably in the horse's mouth

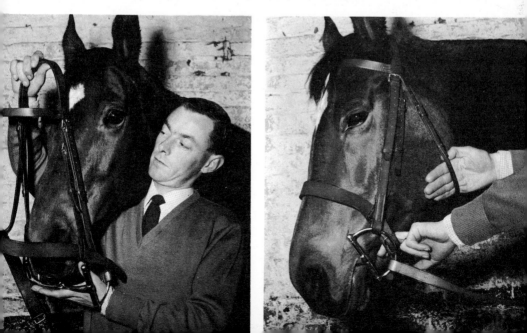

cheek, take the bit with your left hand, place your left thumb between the upper part of his lips, press down on the lower jaw, so asking the horse to open his mouth, then with your left fingers *gently* push the bit into his mouth. Whilst this is going on, your right hand is placing the bridle over the horse's ears; be very careful not to pinch them. The bridle now being in place on his head, you must do up the various buckles. First, the throat latch should be loose enough for you to be able to pass your hand behind it. Second, the noseband: you should be able to get two fingers between it and the horse's face. Third, check that the bit is not too high nor too low in the horse's mouth. Finally, go over the whole thing again and check thoroughly that there are no twisted straps, that all straps are in their keepers, and that the horse is showing no signs of discomfort to your fitting.

MARTINGALES AND THE BREASTPLATE

There are two basic types of martingale, the standing martingale and the running martingale. One important thing to remember here is that the martingale is an artificial aid to the rider, not a part of the horse's saddlery. I stress this because I want you, from the very beginning, to take it for granted that a well trained horse should never require a martingale. The object of the martingale is to prevent the horse from putting his head up too high, to stop him from stargazing by the use of leather restrictions. There is a drawback to both. The standing martingale, which restricts the horse from the noseband, can have a weakening effect on the neck muscles. The running martingale, which restricts the horse from the reins, has a tendency to interfere with the mouth, because of its attachment to the reins.

For competition work, particularly point-to-pointing, cross country riding, in fact all jumping, hunting and fast riding, the horse should always wear a breastplate. Even the best saddles can slip when under great strain, and the breastplate, as illustrated, is the rider's and the horse's safety strap.

If your mount is not happy and comfortable in his "tack" you will never work together as a happy and unified team, and this should be the aim of all who ride.

34

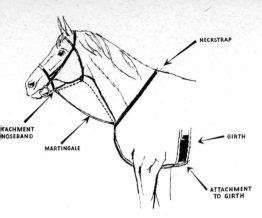

The standing martingale

The dotted lines show the line the martingale should follow if fitted correctly

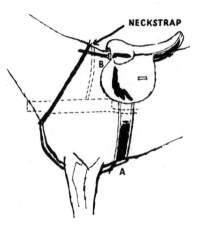

The running martingale

The dotted lines show the position of the breastgirth
A *The union with the girth*
B *The union with the saddle*

Having now gained this knowledge of the equipment, the next step is to learn how to fit it onto your mount. All this should be part of your riding instruction.

IF A MARTINGALE IS REQUIRED

The standing martingale should be fitted so that you are able to trace the contours of the horse's neck with the strap. Check that the strap is not pinching where it joins the girth. The running martingale should be fitted so that when the rings are unattached from the reins; one should be able to touch the withers with both rings. Again check that it will not chafe at its union with the girth.

Remember, at all times, the horse's comfort comes first: yours comes next.

5 Equitation

I WANT YOU TO IMAGINE that I am going to take you on a riding course. We will go from stage to stage, and phase to phase. The ultimate aim of the course is to produce a rider capable of riding with a high degree of safety and comfort for his horse, to be able to enjoy himself, and ready to become, with experience and the correct guidance, what should be the aim of us all—a horseman.

The terms elementary, intermediate and advanced are descriptive only of the course, not to any particular standard of equitation. Unless I could actually see you mounted, it would be impossible for me to judge any standard of riding that you may reach.

INTRODUCTION

PHASE ONE: This would normally include an introduction to the horse as an animal, which was covered in Chapter One. Your very first lesson will not be a lesson at all, it will purely be a "getting the feel" ride. You will go on a leading rein, and the idea will be to get you to relax thoroughly, to get used to sitting on a living animal, and for you and me, as pupil and instructor, to discuss what is going to happen to you on future lessons. It does not matter to me if you stand on your head on the horse's back, providing you come back from this ride, having enjoyed yourself, and with a desire to learn to ride to the best of your ability!

PHASE TWO: Now we start the instruction proper, and the first thing you have to learn is how to lead your horse, when unmounted. If you are going to lead the horse for some distance, then the reins should not be over his neck, but if it is only a short distance then you can leave the reins over his neck. Hold the reins in your right hand, approximately four inches from the bit, dividing the two reins with your index finger. The remainder of the reins should be held in your left hand. Do not be tempted to twist the reins around your wrist or hand, because if the horse jumped away from you this could be very dangerous. There should be no need physically to drag the horse along, he should walk quite willingly with you. Now we have got to

Leading the horse with the reins over his head

Leading the horse when in a head collar
(The head collar is for use in the stable or when travelling)

Leading the horse with the reins on his neck

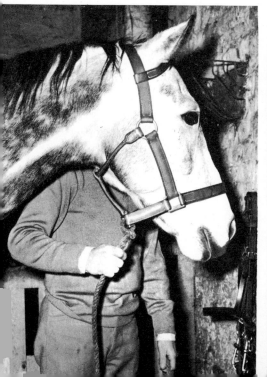

get you on to the horse. Remember you are not going to look silly if you do something wrong; you are bound to do something wrong. The horse has been especially picked for the job because of his patient and placid nature. Don't think it is going to be an all-in wrestling match to get you into the "boat". Approach your mount as described earlier; then take the reins in your left hand, with the left rein entering your hand from under your little finger, and the right from between your index finger and thumb. Adjust the right rein slightly shorter than the left; some horses are apt to give a playful nip whilst being mounted. The reins should be of sufficient length to restrict the horse from walking forward. Turn and face the horse's tail, placing your left shoulder next to your mount's shoulder. Take the stirrup iron in your right hand, and place your left foot into the iron. Stretch up and place your right hand over the waist of the saddle. During this time your left hand is purely resting on the front of the saddle; it is not your left hand that gets you up but your right. Now spring from your right foot, and by using your right hand swing yourself gently into the saddle. It is most important that you take very great care not to dig your mount in the ribs with your left toe, and that you do actually arrive *gently* into the saddle. Once arrived, then you can place your right foot into the right stirrup iron. The stirrup leathers should be turned so that they lie flat against your lower shin bone.

You must now take up the reins in both hands. They should be held with the rein entering your hand between the little finger and the third finger, and leaving between the thumb and the index finger. Their position should be roughly four inches above the horse's withers, that is about the base of his neck, and roughly six inches apart. The hands should always be parted, and they should be in what is called the carried position, that is to say you must never lean your hands upon your horse's neck or the saddle. They, and their weight, should always be carried by you.

I have assumed, and will assume throughout, that the horse has a single reined bridle. I feel it is so easy to make the whole operation terribly complicated on paper. By dealing with a single rein only, I sincerely hope that I will be able to give you as much information as possible, as simply as possible.

The first stage of mounting

The second stage of mounting. Note the position of the left toe

All these three positions have been specially posed

The third stage of mounting: arriving in the saddle

To shorten the length of rein whilst mounted, take the right rein between your left forefinger and thumb, then slide the right hand to the length you require, repeat the operation with your left hand. Do not grab at the reins with your right hand and then with your left, it will startle your mount and worry him. All your movements whatever they may be, and no matter what circumstances they are made in, should be gentle, smooth and definite. It is through the reins that your mount gets his "feel" of you, and it is through your hands that you get your "feel" of him. Your hands are your transmitter and the reins are the horse's receiver. Try to imagine that you are holding two very wet sponges, and each time you pull or squeeze on them you only wish to let a drop of water out at a time, and not all of it at once! The reins are there for you to hold and use, *not* for you to hang on by.

To my mind, the mark of a well trained rider is to be able to adjust his length of rein, his length of stirrup leather, and his girth, without the whole world knowing about it or noticing it has been done. You adjust your stirrup leather by using your forefinger and thumb, without looking down, and with your foot remaining in the stirrup iron.

How to hold the reins on a single rein bridle

First and second stages of dismounting
These positions have been specially posed

To tighten your girth, or to loosen it, gently move your left leg forward, lift the saddle flap with your left hand, the reins being in your right, hold the flap up with your right hand, and by using again your (left) forefinger and thumb, tighten or loosen the girth. Do not look down.

"What goes up must come down", so to dismount, take both feet out of the irons, lean forward on to the horse's neck, and *gently* vault off. Do not try to dismount with one foot remaining in an iron, or by swinging your right leg over the horses neck. One does see these methods used far too often, but if the horse were to be startled they could be very dangerous. There is nothing clever in doing things the dangerous way with horses, as the horse is generally the sufferer.

PHASE THREE: You can now mount and dismount. The next step is your position in the saddle, ready for what we are going to do once the horse is in motion. I want you to place yourself into the middle and lowest part of the saddle, then position your legs so that there is an imaginary line from your heels to your hips to your shoulders, keeping also your toe in line with your knee. Place your weight on your heels and press the heels down; your toes should be very slightly turned outwards, and you should have contact with the saddle from your upper thighs to the lower part of your calf. The upper part of your body should be slightly leaning forward, just off the upright, your chest open, your head erect, and your elbows in. At the walk your hips and the small of your back should move easily and naturally with the movements of the horse.

The basic principles of the seat are balance, rhythm, and grip. I purposely place grip last, and a very poor last. You must not ride on grip. This should only be used as a "safety valve" if all else fails, for instance when jumping tricky obstacles, if your mount should buck or be startled, and as a last resort, to keep your seat. The whole secret of good riding is to be supple and relaxed, so that you are able to move naturally with the rhythm of the horse. If you are relying purely on grip, then your muscles are tight and hard, and I do not believe that anybody can relax and grip at the same time. A well trained rider should ride on balance and rhythm 95% of the time, judiciously using grip only when it is needed.

You can encourage this suppleness by doing simple exercises. Here is one exercise: Place the reins in your right hand, then with your left hand bend down and touch your right toe, repeat this four times. Whilst doing this exercise remember to try to keep your lower body in contact with the saddle. The second exercise is what I call a "side saddle exercise" (it has nothing to do with riding side-saddle). Place your right or left leg over the front of your saddle, hold the reins with both hands, then at the walk just relax the base of your spine and allow it to move freely with the motion of your mount. You will not be able to keep a stiff back in this position for very long.

Note here, by the way, you are still on the LEADING rein or the LUNGEING rein.

ELEMENTARY

This stage will deal with the actual movements of the horse, and how you should sit at each one. Some elementary control will also be covered.

PHASE ONE: There are two types of trot, the sitting trot and the rising trot. The sitting trot is what it says, one sits down in the saddle and moves in rhythm with the horse. This can become very comfortable, and it is very important that you practise it every time you ride. When changing direction, trotting over uneven ground, or increasing and decreasing the pace, you must sit down into your saddle. This is so that you may have as close a contact as possible with your mount. These changes of pace are called transitions.

The trot is a two-beat rhythm. The horse's legs move diagonally, that is the left front leg goes forward as the right hindleg goes forward, and the right foreleg as the left hindleg goes forward. In the rising trot you must rise up and down in time with the two beats. You must not under any circumstances use the reins to pull yourself up and down. Now you are going to find this very uncomfortable at first, but once you have got "the hang of it" it should not require any physical effort on your or the horse's part. You will get plenty of time to practise this, but I want you to keep in the back of your mind, at all times, that as you return to the saddle, you are coming down upon a living spine as sensitive as your own. So try to go up and down gently. Do not be tempted to stand up in your irons, just go up and down as if you were getting out of a chair. In the opening strides of your trot, and in the closing, sit down into your saddle, thus maintaining contact until the horse is in his stride or stops.

Having mastered the going up and down, and the sitting trot, I want you now to stop and start your mount. (Remember you are still on the leading rein or the lungeing rein.) To start, first shorten your reins, then draw your legs into the horse in a squeezing action and push down and forward with your seat bones. If your horse does not answer to this, and riding school horses can get "cheesed off" with their jobs the same as you, then give him a firm but slight kick with your heels. If possible, though, try to avoid having to do this. Given time and the correct experience you will eventually be able to get your mount to increase or decrease his pace at your suggestion. To stop, or slow down, all I want you to do at this stage is to pull evenly on both reins, sit down in your saddle and give the command to the horse, W-A-L-K.

43

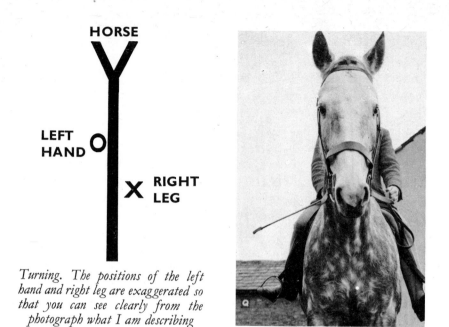

HORSE

LEFT HAND

RIGHT LEG

Turning. The positions of the left hand and right leg are exaggerated so that you can see clearly from the photograph what I am describing

Use your voice as much as possible, as it is one of the most important methods of communication you have with the animal. From the tone of your voice the horse will know whether you are serious about your intentions or not. You can soothe, encourage, correct, with your voice. You will find that horses, particularly riding school horses, are expert psychologists; he will "weigh" you up, before you "weigh" him up!

Your length of rein at all times should be such that you can feel the horse's mouth at the other end. Never, never ride with a loose rein.

At this phase I would put you off the leading rein or lunge rein, and give you as much practice as possible to perfect what has been covered so far, adding to it an exercise in changing direction, just simple zig-zagging and turning. Again, all I want you to do at this stage of your control training, is to pull on the left rein to go left, and the right rein to go right.

Not until you and I are fully satisfied with things so far will we attempt to canter.

PHASE TWO: Well, you are obviously an apt pupil, so let's get down to work on the canter. For this you will return to the leading rein, or the lunge rein. The canter is a movement of three beats. The idea here is that the rider moves with a rocking action, keeping as close a contact as possible with the saddle. You push forward with your seat bones as the horse strides forward and let the base of your spine move back as the horse brings his legs under him. It is just as if you were pushing a swing higher, or making a rocking horse rock—in fact, you can practise this movement very effectively on a rocking horse. I have found that the best way to teach a rider to canter is to get him to do so without the use of irons. This is not nearly as difficult as it sounds and it is the only way to illustrate the movement of the horse and the position of the rider.

Once you are comfortable at the canter, and I am satisfied with your seat, you will then be given practice lessons in asking your mount to canter. Up to this point your mount has been asked to canter through the lead rein and the lead horse. First you trot, and then on the command

Here is Scampi with the near fore leading and the near hind following suit

Scampi leading with the off fore, with the hind again following suit

Author's note. You will notice that Scampi has changed his head position in these two photographs. This is because he is a young horse that we have in training and has yet to learn his job completely: but his bright colour was what the photographer wanted as we were short of sunshine!

"Canter" you must sit down in your saddle, push with your seat bones and squeeze the horse with your legs. Keep a contact with the horse's mouth at all times through the reins. On the command "Trot" you should close your fingers, push with your seat bones, give your mount the command: "T-R-O-T". Keep the pressure on the reins until the horse trots; once he does, open your fingers and relieve the pressure.

This must be practised—trot, canter, trot, canter, etc. until your execution of the movement is perfect.

PHASE THREE: When the horse is cantering he takes a longer stride with one leg (front and behind), than he does with the other. This longer striding leg is the leading leg. If the leading hindleg is not in unison with the leading foreleg, then the horse is said to be cantering disunited. Don't worry about this sort of thing at this juncture, it will only complicate things: just recognise it and appreciate it. You are the pupil, therefore your mount should be sufficiently schooled to answer to your aids correctly, providing, of course, that you are applying the aids correctly.

If you are doing circle work, or riding along twisting forest paths etc., then the ability to control which leg your horse will lead with will be an advantage. For instance, when turning to the left at the canter, if you can control your mount to canter with his near (left) for leading, then he will turn more evenly, with better balance, and suppleness.

To canter on the near fore, press with both legs, but stronger with your right than your left, push with your seat bones, and your mount will strike off with his near fore leading—we hope! To change from the near fore leading to the off fore leading whilst actually in the canter first *return to the trot for three to four paces!* then strike off with the off fore leading. The aids for the off fore leading are precisely the opposite from the near fore leading. Never attempt to change from the near to the off without first returning to the trot.

Off the leading rein you go again, and practise—practise. When you and I are completely satisfied—completely—then you will be off the rein for good.

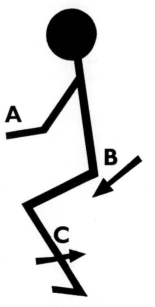

Transition from a slow pace to a faster one, and from a fast pace to a slower one

Note. When going from a fast pace to a slower, i.e. canter to trot, it is exactly the same process, but more resistance with the hands and the impulsion should be kept at all paces

A *Close the fingers*
B *Push down with the seat bones*
C *Squeeze with the legs*

PHASE FOUR: The gallop and faster riding is the main theme of this phase. The gallop is of very little importance to your education at the moment, but it is good, mentally, for the novice rider to experience it. You will never forget that terrific, elated feeling of your first gallop. In the gallop, you lean forward more than in the other paces, and slightly raise your "bottom" out of the saddle, but need to take care not to let the reins go loose. The remainder of this phase will be to gain as much experience as possible with just general riding.

This is where you might take your first tumble, if you haven't already done so. Try not to worry about falling off; it is certainly no disgrace. (In fact some children regard it as a battle honour!) Falling off is a natural part of riding, we all fall off. My one dread is that one day I will fall off in front of a class of children (and adults!). You stand far less chance of falling off a horse and hurting yourself, than you do of hurting yourself when crossing the road or driving.

INTERMEDIATE

PHASE ONE: The natural aids are the voice, the hands, the legs, and the seat. The voice I have placed first for the reasons explained in Phase One, for Elementary. The hands are our means of interpretation, feel, and control. They are in fact, another way of talking to the horse.

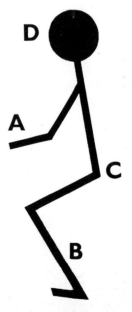

The natural aids

A *The hands—control pace, direction. Through them we get our feel and interpretation*
B *The legs—control pace and direction and create impulsion*
C *Seat, balance—create impulsion and rhythm*
D *The voice—can do practically anything*

It is through the hands that we control pace, direction, and balance. The legs also give the signals to control the pace, direction, and balance. The seat (this time I mean your seat bones and upper thighs) create impulsion, or putting it another way one encourages, by pushing downwards with the seat bones, the energy of the horse and puts it to use. Eventually, I repeat eventually, you will be able to use aids independently, and when necessary all at the same time. Do not worry if you find this difficult; it does take time and practice.

Before going on to the actual execution of these aids, you must get some understanding of what we mean by collection. The British Horse Society Manual of Horsemanship defines collection thus: "Collection is the concentration of the horse's energy, when the whole of his body is collected into a shortened form with a relaxed jaw, on a light rein, with even more active hind legs, so that he has maximum control over his limbs and is in a position to obey instantly the slightest indication of his rider".

To collect your mount up, first shorten your reins, (not tighten, shorten) push downwards with your seat bones, squeeze your legs into the horse. The squeeze must not be permanent, release the squeeze the moment he walks forward, but keep the pushing of your seat bones and your lower spine. You are asking the horse to "collect himself", so remember that the energy comes from behind—his

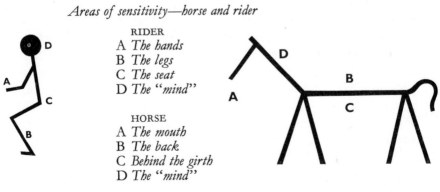

Areas of sensitivity—horse and rider

RIDER
A *The hands*
B *The legs*
C *The seat*
D *The "mind"*

HORSE
A *The mouth*
B *The back*
C *Behind the girth*
D *The "mind"*

49

engine is at the back. Imagine the horse is a car; whilst relaxing he is in neutral, when collected, you have put his engine into gear, and he is ready to answer your "asking". Again you will not learn this overnight, so do not get despondent if you do not understand at first, or you are not successful at first in executing it. Given time, you will succeed.

During an actual lesson, try to have your horse collected all the time. Remember, though that whilst your mount is collected he is using energy, therefore it is tiring for him. On your way back to the stables, or after the lesson allow him to stretch and move his neck fairly freely—in other words let him relax.

PHASE TWO: To get you using the aids, most of this phase will be exercises in stopping, starting, and turning. So let us go through each exercise and analyse your application of the aids.

Starting: First shorten the rein, not tighten, squeeze with your legs, and push with your seat bones and the small of your back. If you get no responce then by bringing your heels in behind the girth, give your mount a short but firm kick. You are not kicking a football; remember, he is a living creature, so don't give him a thump in the ribs.

Stopping: Sit well down into your saddle, apply an even pressure on *both* reins, push with your seat, and bring your horse to an even halt. This also applies to slowing from a faster pace to a slower one, i.e. canter to the trot, trot to the walk. Do not tug on the reins, and yell "Wo".

Turning: To turn your mount to the right, apply pressure on the right rein and press your left leg just behind the girth. Whilst executing this, you should be sitting well down in your saddle, thus keeping a close contact with the horse. In turning, the curve of the horse's neck must not be greater than the curve of his body. If it is then you are pulling him round physically and not through the ability of your technique. The legs are used to control the hindquarters. On the turn your mount's hindquarters must not swing outwards, but follow the track of the forelegs. The opposite hand to the direction in which you are turning is controlling the degree of the turn you are making. To turn to the left is, of course, vice versa.

Whilst practising these movements we will also be working on your control of pace, that is keeping the horse at a steady and rhythmic movement, and under control at all times.

Remember whilst making a transition from one pace to another, always sit well into your saddle. Try to make your transitions definite, fluent, and stylish. For example, do not put your mount into a canter by first doing such a fast trot that the poor animal can do nothing else but break into a canter.

ADVANCED

PHASE ONE: Now we have got to make your riding more artistic, and perhaps a little scientific. In this phase you are going to learn how to change the diagonal, the leading leg at the canter.

First the changing of the diagonals. The horse whilst trotting moves diagonally, that is, his left foreleg goes forward as his right hindleg goes forward, and vice versa. Now at the walk, rise up and down so that you return to the saddle as the left shoulder comes back. Your mount is now carrying your weight on his left diagonal, so if you were trotting you would be on the left diagonal. Now at the trot practise rising up and down, so that you return to the saddle as the left shoulder comes back—and there you are trotting away on the left diagonal.

For the right diagonal, reverse the exercises and use the right shoulder. Do not worry at this stage about looking down at the horse's shoulders. Later, given the correct practice, you will be able to recognise which diagonal you are on without looking down.

Now for the actual change. First trot on, and when I say "change", sit down in your saddle, miss one stride and start rising again. What you have done is to change your weight from one side of the horse to the other. What are the advantages? If you were carrying a suitcase to the station, or a shopping bag down the High Street, you would find it less of a strain if you changed it from time to time from one hand to the other; what is more, you could carry it comfortably for a longer distance. Well, in changing your diagonals that is what you are doing for your mount. You are making life easier, more comfortable and less of a strain. You are not altering the strides of the horse in any way. You are merely changing your weight from one side to the other. Change the diagonal as often as possible.

Changing the diagonals is in my opinion far more important than the correct leading leg at the canter. With the latter the horse, if he so wishes, can freely change the support of your weight by changing from the near fore leading to the off fore leading. In the trot the horse cannot alter the support of your weight, but you can—by changing the diagonal! This is very important when riding cross-crountry, pony trekking, hunting, or any long periods of trotting.

PHASE TWO: This would be a complete revision of everything covered so far—practise, practise, practise! At this phase you should now start hiding your aids. Imagine that your father, mother or a friend, is watching you ride. Afterwards, when you dismount, if they say to you, "That looks so easy. I'm sure I could do it. I didn't see you move", then you know you are well on the way to becoming a horse-man.

Riding is not a test of courage, it is a test of skill. Like the ballet, riding is an art, the complete harmony of rhythm and movement between man and beast.

I have tried throughout this chapter to avoid being too "text book-ish"; whilst you can learn from a book, you cannot possibly learn to ride from it. I have tried to lay before you the basic facts and fundamentals of how to ride the horse, and I sincerely hope, in a compre-hensible manner. I have purposely left out many more intricate "school" movements, such as special types of turns etc. Many excellent books have been written on these matters, one of the finest being the British Horse Society's *Manual of Horsemanship*.

Keep in the back of your mind, you are learning to ride to enjoy yourself. Relax and do just that. Indeed given the secret ingredient, time, you will not even mind falling off occasionally!

6 Jumping

ALTHOUGH THERE ARE DIFFERENT TYPES OF JUMPING—steeplechasing, show jumping—the basic seat and technique is more or less the same. The ultimate aim is also the same, that is to encourage the horse to jump, fluently, accurately, and happily. It is no use just going at a jump and hanging on with everything you've got.

The horse is not a natural jumper. The cat and the dog are; they have less ribs than the horse, giving them more suppleness, and soft paws to cushion their weight on landing. Like us the horse has to be trained to jump—to use a definite technique—i.e. we use the Western Roll or Scissors, but unlike us the horse has to carry the extra burden of a man on his back over obstacles. The rider, therefore, must study and strive to perfect a good jumping technique, so that he does not interfere with his mount whilst performing.

The rider must control pace, direction, and impulsion, so it makes one's sense of rhythm and speed very important. We control the pace by using our hands, seat, and legs, together or independently. With the hands the rider can steady the pace, or correct the direction. With the seat the rider can increase the pace and create the impulsion (energy) needed to carry the horse over the jump. This is done by sitting down into the saddle, and pushing with the seat bones. By using the legs the rider can control direction. For example, if the horse is moving across to the right of the jump the rider, by pressing with his right leg, can correct it. The legs are also used with the seat to increase pace, and create impulsion.

The position of the rider

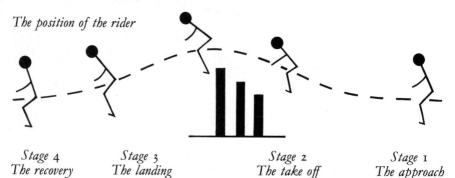

| *Stage 4* | *Stage 3* | *Stage 2* | *Stage 1* |
| The recovery | The landing | The take off | The approach |

The horse's neck and head are his natural balancing pole, and in jumping the rider must allow the horse to use them freely. The hands must follow the line of the neck. They must not interfere with the mouth, in any way, once the horse has begun his flight. Because of this great care must be taken to ensure that the rider's seat is, naturally, completely independent of the reins, before commencing any jumping training.

There are four main stages of jumping.

1 The Approach   2 The Take Off
3 The Flight and Landing   4 The Recovery or Next Approach

THE APPROACH

STAGE ONE: The approach must be straight and calm, with the rider and the horse looking exactly where they are going, and aiming at the middle of the obstacle. Once the rider knows where the jump is, then he should try to look beyond it and not directly at it. On the approach the rider should be controlling pace and direction.

THE TAKE OFF

STAGE TWO: On nearing the fence the rider must sit well down into the saddle, and by using this seat and legs, "ask" the horse to jump. The hands must be kept well down, and move with the forward movement of the horse, allowing him to use his head and neck freely. As the horse actually leaves the ground the rider lifts his weight out of the saddle, by leaning forward, keeping his head up, and "cushioning" his weight on his thighs, legs, ankles, and heels. The heels must still be kept down. He should have a light and flexible contact with the horse's mouth.

The Take Off

THE FLIGHT AND LANDING

STAGE THREE: The rider must still keep his position forward with the movement of the horse, taking his weight on his thighs and ankles. As the horse begins to land, then the rider must gradually regain contact with the saddle. A good guide in jumping is to try and keep a line from the horse's bit, through the hands to the elbow.

THE RECOVERY OR NEXT APPROACH

STAGE FOUR: Having sighted his next jump, the rider must now control the pace and direction, as in Stage One, and in so doing give his mount plenty of time also to sight his next obstacle.

The Recovery

THE DON'TS OF JUMPING

Here the rider has lost contact with the horse's mouth, has moved too far forward in the saddle, and seems to be relying on the knee grip and nothing else. The complete picture is one of disharmony and frustration on the part of the horse

Here the rider has again moved too far forward, but this time the upper part of the body only, thus pushing the elbows out and making the legs too stiff

Here is one of the most common mistakes made in jumping. The rider has attempted to lean back whilst landing, thus forcing himself to hang on to the horse's mouth, and again forcing his legs to straighten. Notice that the horse's hind quarters have started to drop before he has completed his jump

Here is a ride nicely spaced out. These learner riders are returning from a lesson

7   Riding Manners

WHENEVER YOU ARE OUT RIDING, or waiting at the bus stop in jodhpurs, you are a representative of what non-riders call—"horsey people". Whatever you do or say, and how you behave, will be noted and remembered, so make sure that you are something more than just a good representative—be a good ambassador also. Do not let yourself become the calf-slapping, "jolly hockeysticks" type of rider; this is not being "horsey".

Having got this off my mind, let me analyse what I mean by riding manners, and what I intend covering in this chapter. By riding manners I mean behaviour towards other riders, other road users, and other users of the countryside. I have attempted to compile a form of "highway code" for riders.

WHILST OUT ON A RIDE WITH A GROUP

1 Do not get too near to the horse in front. Keep roughly one length away, that is about four feet.
2 Do not make clicking noises with your tongue whilst riding near others. You may mean it for your mount, but it could upset the mounts of others.
3 Do not wave your crop or whip around, especially near the heads of horses.
4 Do not shout or raise your voice.

OUT ON A RIDE ON YOUR OWN

1 Have respect for the countryside and country folk. Have a bright "Good Morning" or "Good Afternoon" for all you meet.
2 Close all gates, and keep out of fields which are sown.
3 Respect all livestock. Go carefully past cattle, sheep, dogs etc. Do not startle them.
4 Try to keep off footpaths, especially when the weather is, or has been, wet. Horses and ponies can make a terrible mess of footpaths when the ground is wet.
5 Be considerate to all you meet, especially very young children, elderly people, wild life, domestic pets. The sudden appearance of a horse, certainly if he is moving fast, could frighten them.
6 Always forewarn other riders if you are approaching them from behind.
7 Never go faster than a walk past other riders unless you have their permission.

WHILST ON THE ROADS

1 Observe and abide by the highway code.
2 Ride as you would (or should) drive, with courtesy and consideration to others.

A ride along a busy road, still well spaced but taking up as little of the road as possible

3 Make allowances for young children, elderly people, and domestic pets.

4 If riding with a group keep in single file whenever possible. Do not leave big gaps in the ride; this can confuse other road users.

5 If you are out early in the morning, do not, unless it is vitally necessary, trot past houses. You may wake someone up, and that someone may be a very hard working night worker.

6 When mounted, keep well into the left.

7 When leading a fresh, or nervous horse, walk on the right hand side of the road, facing the oncoming traffic.

8 Give clear and concise hand signals.

Hand signals

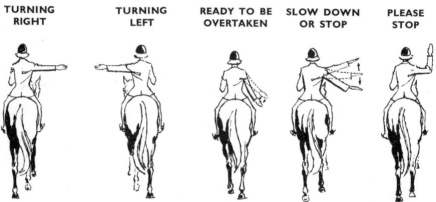

| TURNING RIGHT | TURNING LEFT | READY TO BE OVERTAKEN | SLOW DOWN OR STOP | PLEASE STOP |

9 Always say "thank you" to all other road users, whether they are helpful or not. If you say "thank you", not sarcastically, to those who are not considerate, you will set them thinking as to why? Very few people are purposely inconsiderate; in many cases it is lack of knowledge.

10 Remember that the horse is a fairly slow moving road user, so allow for impatience on the part of other road users and try to tolerate it.

11 Be nice to all road users, even the grumpy ones!

12 In heavy traffic, now and again make a fuss of your mount; let him see you are not nervous, even if you are, and that he is not alone.

13 When riding along narrow lanes, pass all others at the walk.
14 If your mount shies, turn his head away from the object and don't look at it yourself.
15 You need not ride in silence, but be alert to traffic conditions.
16 On slippery or icy roads, dismount and lead.
17 Never get separated whilst crossing a main road or a road junction.
18 Obey all police, traffic control signals, and traffic lights
19 Do not assume that because you are a horse lover and are familiar with them, everybody else is as well.

WHILST AT THE STABLES

1 Pass the time of day with the staff by all means, but do not get too familiar with them. They have a job to do and chatting to you may land them in trouble.
2 Don't rush up to the horse in his box, with arms outstretched and calling sweet endearments to him. He may rush back into the box and slip, or knock his head.
3 Do not lean on stable doors or stable equipment, i.e., brooms, pitch forks etc.

Do not give the horses tit-bits unless you have permission

4 Treat all saddlery as if it were your own.

5 Do not lead any horses out of their boxes until shown how to do it, and unless asked to do so.

6 Do not go into any horse in his box without permission.

7 Enjoy your visits as much as you can, but keep your voice and laughter down.

8 Be careful with cigarettes and matches.

9 If you have to cancel your ride, try to give the instructor as much notice as you can.

10 Behave at the stables as you would at home.

11 Do not give the horses tit-bits unless you have permission.

WHILST AT A HORSE SHOW

1 If you are hacking to the show, do not gallop madly along grass verges. Many local councils forbid riding on grass verges, and in the majority of cases the riders have only themselves to blame for this rule.

2 At the show, or whatever function it may be, do not "warm up" your mount near the collecting ring, the main ring, the spectators or any trade stands.

3 Try not to get too excited, try to keep calm and be considerate to all around you.

4 Again do not assume that all at a "horsey function" are knowledge-able; although they may enjoy watching them perform, they might be nervous of them at close quarters.

5 Do not canter or jump near other stationary horses and ponies, especially if they are unmounted.

6 Avoid anything that is likely to startle spectators or other animals.

7 Be dressed correctly if you are competing.

In all cases put the horse first and yourself last; behave to him in the way you would expect to be treated yourself.

8   Riding Activities

HAVING LEARNT THE BASIC RUDIMENTS OF RIDING, what are you going to do with this new found talent and enjoyment? There are so many ways that one can enjoy the horse—hunting, show jumping, polo, etc.—it is almost endless. He is almost over-generous, there is so much that we can do, on him, with him, whatever our incomes. Thank heavens the horse has no trade union! Riding activity can mean not only active participation in competitions, but also tremendous enjoyment for active spectators. Add to this the fact that you can watch, admire, follow and enjoy, the horse for every month of the year. In winter there is steeplechasing, point-to-point, hunting, combined training events, and hunter trials. At Christmas we go to the pantomime or circus, and what do we see? Horses. In the spring there is steeplechasing, flat racing, pony racing, show jumping, horse shows, three day events, driving marathons, and polo, going on right up to the following winter. At the summer military tattoos and tournaments. What do we see? The horse. If you dream of becoming a famous rider, then the horse offers you many different ways in which you can try to make your dream come true. If you ever do fulfil that dream, don't forget it was thanks to the horse.

Hunting begins about the beginning of November and ends about March. The hunting field is not a competition, not officially anyway, but from the hunting field have come some of our top cross-country riders, steeplechase jockeys, and show jumping riders. It is perhaps the quickest way of learning how to look after your mount, and yourself, whilst riding and jumping with others and at speed. It is also, perhaps, the quickest way of getting to know yourself! You can either buy or hire a hunter; in all hunting areas there are stables with fit, experienced hunters for hire at quite reasonable prices. Before going hunting you should first become a member of the local hunt. This is expensive, but when you consider what you are getting in return, it is well worth it. Before taking this step you should have observed two very important items, they are:

*The author on his
Grade A Showjumper
Signalman, White
City, 1965*

1 Take a special course in riding for hunting. Nearly all hunting areas have stables that run such courses. It is not enough to take a short course in jumping; hunting is cross country riding, and calls for special techniques.

2 Learn, read, and completely memorise the rules and etiquette of the hunting field. You will drop a terrible "clanger" if you break these. The British Horse Society will always be willing to advise, and they also publish pamphlets on the subject.

A good introduction is to follow the hunt on foot or by motor car. This will give you an idea of the sort of country you can expect to ride over, and an off-stage view of the system of the hunt.

Show jumping is a sport which can be participated in on a modest scale and budget, but you nearly always show a loss at the end of the season—still you are in it for a hobby. It can be one of the most thrilling and satisfying of pastimes. Your first step is to join the British Show Jumping Association; this you must do if you wish to compete in recognised shows. If you own your own horse or pony, then you must register him also with the Association. Should you not be lucky enough to own your own mount, it is still possible to compete in equestrian events by joining the Pony Club or a Riding Club, but more of this later.

Before competing in show jumping make a very careful study of the art. For show jumping calls for special techniques and accurate judgement of pace. If you can afford it, as with hunting, take a special course in show jumping riding.

64

Show jumping is by no means the only way of showing. There are events for hacks, working hunters, cobs, hackneys, and dressage competitions. For those not quite so seriously minded there are mounted games, fancy dress competitions etc. All of these *can* be done on a modest scale and on a modest budget, and give you in return a great deal of fun and exciting stories to tell in your old age.

Polo is, perhaps, the most expensive of horsey pastimes. If you can afford it, then polo can be an exciting sport to take as your hobby. There are now in this country many first class polo stables, specialising purely in the training of polo players and the schooling of polo ponies. If you base your dream on becoming a star player, then take a long, cold, sober look at your bank statement first.

One of the most outstanding features of equestrian sports is the fact that they are all open to male and female competitors. Both sexes can take part on absolutely equal terms, and as much as we males hate admitting it, ladies win very, very frequently. Furthermore there are competitions for juniors and adults. I cannot think offhand (in fact I don't want to!) of any sport that offers all these advantages.

Three day eventing is a combination of dressage (a test in flexibility and obedience), show jumping, steeplechasing and cross country riding. It is in fact the supreme test of horse and rider. If you can compete

Lt. Col. Frank Weldon riding Fermoy over an obstacle while competing in the Badminton Horse Trials

Polo at Cowdray Park

Mrs. V. D. S. Williams on her famous dressage horse, Little Model

Steeplechasing at Cheltenham

in these with even moderate success, then you can claim to be a horseman. It is a sport, though, that is very demanding, calling for a great deal of intensive training. Therefore you must have plenty of spare time, and money. Don't despair though; many riding clubs and pony club branches run one day events and two day events, little three day events, which the average rider, working on a small budget, can enter.

For a real man's sport nothing, I feel, can equal amateur steeplechase racing. The word "man" I use in a purely descriptive sense, as this, like everything else in the horsey world, is open to women also. You do not have to be a millionaire to enjoy amateur racing. But you do have to be tough for falls are frequent, injuries are frequent, but the excitement and fun is endless.

One of the best ways of getting started as an amateur steeplechase jockey is to compete in point-to-point racing. These are race meetings organised by the local hunts, with open races, ladies' races and members' only races. From this you can progress to what are called hunter chases. These are part of the race card at many famous racecourses under the control of the National Hunt Committee, the governing body of steeplechasing in this country. Most of our top flight jumping jockeys started their professional careers as amateurs. It is by no means impossible for you to become one of them.

If you cannot partake in point-to-pointing, and you live fairly near a racecourse training centre or a training establishment, go along and see the trainer, tell him you are keen on becoming an amateur jockey. New young talent is always given a helping hand in this business. Ask him if you can ride out exercise for him each day. If you are good the trainer may allow you to ride schooling over practice hurdles and fences. If you are really good he may give you some spare rides on the racecourse proper. After that only you can prove just how good you are; competition is strong. Should you not have enough talent to race, then the trainer has got a useful "spare" exercise rider, and you have found an interesting hobby helping to train racehorses.

The Grand National has been won by amateur jockeys—perhaps you are the next—it's possible!

Along with polo, I would put the breeeding of horses among the most expensive ways of enjoying the horse. It is a very specialised field, and unless you are really confident you know what you are doing, do not dabble in it. The expenses are high, the results a gamble. Again, if you are wealthy, then breeding horses can offer you a fascinating hobby.

*Some foals in the paddock at Col. C. B. R. Hornung's
stud at Cowfold, Sussex*

A Pony Club rally

For those under twenty-one there is the Pony Club. This is an international club, which embraces all forms of riding activity at a cost within the reach of practically everybody. It is here that the owner rider and the non-owning rider can compete together and thoroughly enjoy themselves. Besides competitions there are rallies, picnic rides, visits to famous stables, visits to important horse shows and visits from equestrian celebrities. Add to this a social life equal to none, and you have all the ingredients for an excellent hobby. At the rallies and camps, qualified instructors are invited to give you instructions and guidance in all aspects appertaining to the horse and riding. Members can take proficiency tests at all standards in equitation, stable and horse management. The British Horse Society will be able to tell you where your nearest branch is. The annual subscription is very modest.

The riding clubs cater for those over twenty-one, and are run on similar lines to the Pony Club. All the best riding clubs are affiliated to the British Horse Society. Here again is where the non-owning rider can compete at very moderate cost. If you have not got a club in your area, then, with the advice of the British Horse Society, why not form one at your office or factory?

Holidays with a difference? We all want these sometimes, and here again the dear old horse fills a need. There are trekking holidays, instructional holidays, and gipsy holidays with a horse and caravan. The whole family can enjoy these holidays from the youngest to grandma, and what better way is there of seeing the countryside than from the back of a horse? You do not have to be an experienced equestrian to go pony trekking. For the more dedicated there are many residential riding schools throughout the country, giving instruction in all forms of equitation. For the more romantic there are holidays in gipsy caravans with your own horse to drive—what could be more romantic than this?

If you are not interested, or not able actively to compete, there is still a great deal of enjoyable activity for you. One can derive a life-long, fascinating hobby in just learning to ride and care for the horse. Learn, learn, and learn again; the deeper you get in the subject, the more exciting it becomes. Ride as often as you can, read books, admire great works of art by equestrian artists, and if possible attend lectures and film shows.

I guarantee you will never be left wanting if you make riding and the horse your hobby.

Trekking in the Lorna Doone Valley, Exmoor

9 Buying Your Own Horse

ALMOST ALL OF US WHO RIDE, dream of owning a horse one day of our own. As a child, it was my regular dream, and I was very lucky because it soon became a reality. For obvious reasons we cannot all own a horse, but for those who are thinking of buying one, or dreaming of buying one, then I hope this chapter will be of help.

Buying a horse is the same as buying a car, insomuch as the costs of keeping it are just as important as the cost of buying. So having decided how much you wish to pay for your mount, you must immediately consider and try to calculate whether you can afford to keep him in good health. There are several ways of accommodating your own horse, but the three most common are:

1 To put him, or her, into livery at a local stable.
2 To keep him at grass.
3 To build your own stable, and look after him yourself.

Perhaps the most economical way of keeping a horse is to put him into a field with good grass. It is not enough, though, to turn the poor fellow out into a field and leave him to look after himself. The field must have plenty of grass and the horse will need some form of shelter. There must also be a tank of some sort, which must be filled each day with fresh water. If the field is near a busy road, then it must be well fenced and the gate must lock securely. Through the winter your horse will need hay to make up for the shortage of grass, and if you intend hunting or competing on him, then he will require regular feeding throughout the year. The horse will need what is called a New Zealand rug during the winter months, particularly between November and February. This is a rug especially designed for horses at grass all the year; it is made in such a way that it is unlikely to move or chafe a horse whilst out at grass.

Your cost headings for keeping a horse or pony at grass would be along these lines:

1 The rent or purchase of field.
2 Feeding costs winter and summer.

3 The horse's clothing.
4 Veterinary costs. Even though your horse may be in perfect health do get the Veterinary Surgeon to give him a check over at least once every six months.
5 Blacksmith costs. Your horse's feet must have expert attention at least once every three weeks.
6 The cost of erecting a shelter (not facing the wind).

At home you should have your saddlery, your grooming equipment, and a medicine chest. Your local veterinary surgeon will advise you on the items needed for your medicine chest.

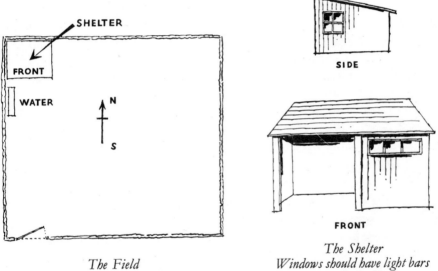

The Field

The Shelter
Windows should have light bars
on the inside

The third method is to build your own stable. If you have a large enough garden, and the neighbours do not mind, then you can have your own stable at the bottom of the garden. Your stable, or loose box, as we call it, should be about 14 ft by 12 ft for a horse, and 12 ft by 10 ft for a pony. It should be light and airy. The horse needs plenty of ventilation, winter and summer, to keep him healthy. For extra warmth in winter, put more rugs on to your horse and do not close up the stable.

71

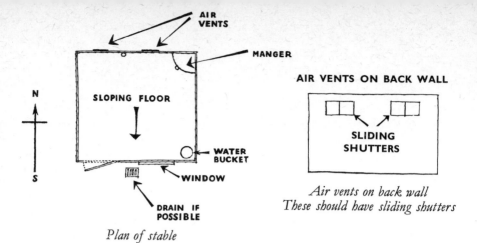

AIR VENTS

MANGER

AIR VENTS ON BACK WALL

N

SLOPING FLOOR

SLIDING
SHUTTERS

S

WATER
BUCKET

WINDOW

DRAIN IF
POSSIBLE

*Air vents on back wall
These should have sliding shutters*

Plan of stable

Stuffy air is not healthy air. Leave the top half of the stable door open winter and summer. The door should be at least 4 ft 6 in in width, it should have two bolts on the bottom portion, preferably of the non-projecting variety. In one corner of the box there should be a manger, and on the wall a ring for tying up the horse whilst grooming and for the securing of a hay net. The floor should be non-slippery, and have a slight slope towards the door to allow drainage.

Your cost headings in this case will be:

1 The cost of erecting a loose box.
2 Stable equipment. i.e. wheelbarrow, broom, pitch fork and shovel.
3 Feeding costs all the year round. You will require some form of covered storage space for feeding stuffs and bedding. Feed bins will be required for oats and bran. The horse will need a hay net, a water bucket, and a feeding bucket.
4 A place to keep your saddlery, medicine chest, and grooming equipment. (This can be kept in the house.)
5 Veterinary costs.
6 Blacksmith's costs.
8 Horse clothing. (i.e. rugs, blankets, etc.)

If you do decide to look after your own horse, then even before buying your horse learn all you can about stable management. If there are any evening classes on horsemastership in your area try and attend them. Read all the books you can on the subject. If the Principal will allow you to help at the riding school during your spare time and holidays, this is valuable experience. *Do not try to learn stable management by*

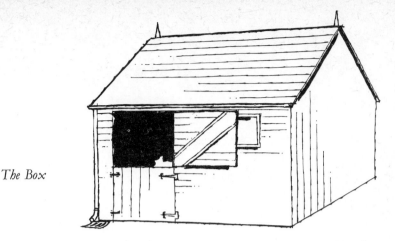

The Box

trial and error—you may learn by your mistakes—but your horse will suffer by them!

I hope I have not made it sound too expensive to keep your own horse, because for what you are getting it is well worth it. By sacrificing a few of life's luxuries, and by careful and efficient budgetting, you do not have to be a millionaire to own your own horse.

Putting a horse or pony at livery means that your horse will become a kind of paying guest at a riding school or livery stable. Here you will only have three main cost headings:

1 Cost of livery per month.
2 Veterinary costs.
3 Blacksmith's costs.

You will be required to supply your own saddlery, horse clothing etc. The stable will be responsible for your horse, his health and happiness, and the cleaning of your saddlery and horse clothing. Check very thoroughly that your horse is going to be well looked after and treated; be as choosey over this as you were over your first riding school, or as you were over last year's family holiday accommodation.

The best and the safest way to buy a horse or pony is through your riding instructor. He knows your personality and he knows your ability, and with this knowledge he can set about buying the right horse for you or the right pony for your child. Tell him how much you wish to pay and leave the rest to him. Amateur horse buyers can be cruel without knowing it.

73

SOME CHILDREN'S PONIES

An example of a good children's pony. Bonny stands about 12 hands 2 inches, and would be suitable for a child 7 to 12 years old

This is also a children's pony, suitable for gymkhana and Pony Club work

A hunter-bred mare who has hunted and is quite a good example of a lady's hack or light weight hunter

A good family type of horse capable of carrying up to 14½ stone. Notice the thick, strong body set on short but strong legs

SOME EQUESTRIAN TERMINOLOGY

or How to Speak "Horsey"

A

ACTION Used to describe the horse in movement, i.e. a horse with good action—a good mover.

AIDS The methods by which the rider conveys his wishes to the horse. Natural aids, the voice, the hands, the legs, the seat. Unnatural aids, the whip, the spur, the martingale, etc.

"ASK" A rider is said to ask his mount when requiring extra effort from him.

B

BALANCE A horse is said to be balanced when his weight and that of his rider are so distributed to allow him to use himself to the maximum ease and efficiency.

BAY Is brown-coloured with black points.

BEDDING There are various types, most common being straw, peat moss, bracken, sawdust.

BIT Fits into the horse's mouth.

BLACK Is black in colour with black points.

BLAZE A broad white mark down the face which extends over the bones of the nose.

BODY BRUSH Part of grooming equipment.

BOG SPAVIN A soft swelling of the hock joint. Located in front of the inner side. Caused by strain.

BONE Measurement taken around the foreleg just below the knee. A hunter with good bone should measure $8\frac{1}{2}$ in. The amount of bone determines the weight the horse's body is capable of carrying.

BONE SPAVIN A bony enlargement on the lower aspect of the inside of the hock.

BOX Stable for horse or pony. A loose box, the horse is loose whilst left alone. Motor box, mechanical conveyance designed for transporting horses.

BRAN Part of the horse's diet.

BRAN MASH A laxative that should be fed to all stabled horses, the evening before rest day. To make—fill a stable bucket two-thirds full of bran, add a handful of oats, pour in boiling water, mix thoroughly, cover with sack, leave to stand until cool enough to eat, then feed in.

BRANDS Indications of previous ownership.

BREAKING IN Term appertaining to the young horse's early training.

BREAST PLATE Part of saddlery, prevents saddle from slipping.

BRIDLE A fitment for the horse's head—holds the bit in place.

BROOD MARE Mare used for breeding purposes.

BROWN Is dark brown or nearly black in colour with brown points.

C

CADENCE The cadence of a horse's stride is said to be the "beat", i.e. trot, a gait of two beats.

CANTER or half gallop. A gait with a three beat rhythm.

CAVALLETTI A type of jump used for training horses and riders.

CHAFF Chopped-up hay, sometimes small amounts of oat straw mixed and green foods mixed in. Adds bulk to the horse's feed, and encourages the horse to chew his feed and not rush (bolt) it.

CHESNUT Ginger or reddish colour. Types of chesnut: light, dark, liver.

CLEVELAND BAY A breed of heavy horse.

CLYDESDALE Breed of heavy horse.

COB An animal with the legs of a pony and the body of a horse. Height usually 15 hands—15.2 h.h.

COLIC A form of constipation suffered by the horse. Can be caused by the horse eating his bedding.

COLLECTION Is the concentration of the horse's energy; he is brought into a shortened form with a relaxed jaw, on a light rein, his hind legs being active, so that he has complete control of himself and is ready to obey his rider's indications.

COLOURED, ODD Horses and ponies of no fixed colour are described as odd-coloured.

COLT A young male horse under the age of three years.

CONNEMARA A breed of pony.

CRIB BITING A nervous habit, when the horse will continually bite his manger or stable door. Usually caused by boredom.

CURB CHAIN Used in conjunction with a double bridle or pelham. Fits into the horse's chin groove.

CURB REIN The lower rein of a double bridle or a Pelham.

CURRY COMB Made of rubber or steel, should only be used to clean the body brush and not to be used actually on the horse.

D

DALES A breed of pony.

DANDY BRUSH Part of the grooming equipment.

DARTMOOR A breed of pony.

DOCK Upper part of horse's tail.

DOG A name given to a dishonest horse.

DRAUGHT horse. A horse used for haulage work.

DRESSAGE A test in flexibility and discipline.

D-RINGED SNAFFLE A type of bit.

DUN Mouse to golden colour, with black points and a dark line along the back.

E

ENTIRE A male horse which has not been gelded.

ERGOT Part of the horse just below the fetlock.

EXERCISE BANDAGES Made of stockinette, approx. 3 in wide. They support the tendons and protect the legs.

EXMOOR A breed of pony.

EXTENDED CANTER The horse extends his neck, lengthens his stride, without getting excited or unbalanced.

EXTENDED TROT The horse lengthens his stride, covering as much ground as possible, without his action getting higher.

EXTENDED WALK The horse should cover as much ground as possible without increasing the regularity of his steps, and without getting excited. The hind feet must touch the ground beyond the footprint of the forefeet.

F

FALSE CANTER A horse is said to be cantering false when cantering in a circle to the left with the off fore leading, and vice-versa.

FAST WORK When a racehorse is tuned up at racing or near racing speed.

FELL A breed of pony.

FETLOCK The joint between the pastern and the cannon bone.

FILLY A female foal up to the age of three years.

FOAL A baby horse of either sex up to the 1st January following birth.

FOREARM The upper part of the front legs.

FOREHAND That part of the horse which is in front of the saddle.

FORELOCK The part of the mane that falls between the ears.

FREE-MOVING A horse which goes willingly, loosely, and freely. Not to be confused with an excited horse.

G

GAG SNAFFLE A type of bit which acts on the corners of the lips.

GALLOP A pace of 4-time rhythm.

GIRTH The fitting that holds the saddle in place.

GREY Types of grey: Iron Grey has black or dark colourings, Light Grey has white hairs showing. A Fleabitten Grey has small dark spots, usually brown in colour. A horse is never accurately described as white.

H

HACK A riding horse.

HACKNEY A high-stepping harness horse.

HALF PASS When the horse moves on two tracks, the outside legs crossing in front of the inside legs.

HALTER A simple form of head gear made of webbing.

HAND Unit of measurement, 4 in.

HANDS A natural aid, to control pace, direction and balance.

HEAD COLLAR A head gear made of leather, much stronger than the halter.

HIGHLAND A breed of pony.

HOCK and point of hock. Part of the horse located on the hind legs.

HOOF PICK Part of the grooming equipment.

HORSE An animal measuring more than 15 hands in height.

HUNTER Not a breed of horse but a type.

L

LEADING REIN A rein, usually made of webbing, for leading one horse from another.

LINSEED A type of foodstuff.

LIPPIZANA An Austrian breed of horse used by the famous Spanish riding school.

LUNGE REIN A long webbing rein measuring about 20 to 25 ft.

M

MAKING A HORSE Term applied to training.

MANE The hair laying over the horse's neck.

MANE COMB Part of the grooming equipment used on the mane.

MARE A female horse over the age of three.

MARTINGALE An artificial aid used to keep the horse's head in the correct position.

MORGAN An American breed of horse.

MOUTHING A term applied to the training of the horse to the bit.

MUZZLE The area around the horse's mouth.

N

NEAR SIDE Left hand side.

NEW FOREST A breed of pony.

NUMNAH A felt pad or saddle.

O

OATS Concentrated feed stuff. Can be fed whole, bruised, or crushed. A good oat should be fat, plump, and clean. There is very little difference between white oats and black oats.

OFF SIDE Right hand side.

P

PALOMINO A North American breed of horse. Known as the "golden horse of the West".

PEAT MOSS A type of bedding.
PELHAM A type of bit.
PERCHERON A breed of heavy horse, originating from France.
PIEBALD Black patches and white.
PINTO A type of horse found in America—the Painted Horse.
POINTS Points of a horse—parts and the names for each one. The "points" of a horse are, the muzzle, tips of the ears, mane and tail and the extremities of the four legs.
PONY An animal measuring under 15 hands.

R

RIG A half-gelded horse.
RISING TROT When the rider rises up and down in the saddle.
ROAN A colour which is a mixture of chestnut or bay and white, or black and white hairs throughout the coat—"strawberry", "bay", or "blue".
ROGUE A dishonest horse.
RUBBER, STABLE A cloth used with the grooming kit.

S

SALT LICK or salt block. Every horse should have a salt block placed in his manger or box, so that he may lick whenever he wishes. If not, salt should be added to all feeds.
SCHOOLING Training young horses.
SEAT A natural aid, i.e. the rider can create impulsion by pushing down on the seat bones. Also means the rider's position in the saddle.
SEATS OF LAMENESS The legs, the shoulders, the hips, and the feet.
SHETLAND A Scottish breed of pony.
SHIRE A breed of heavy horse. The tallest and the heaviest in England. Referred to by historians as the "Great Horse of England".
SITTING TROT When the rider sits down in the saddle, e.g. when going from one pace to another.

SKEWBALD A horse which is white with any other colour except black.
SNAFFLE A type of bit.
SNIP White mark between the nostrils.
SOCK White marking on the legs reaching approximately to the fetlock.
SPONGE Part of the grooming equipment.
STALLION Male horse used for breeding.
STALLS Accommodation for horses and ponies in which they remain tied up all the time.
STAR White mark on the forehead.
STOCKING A white leg as far as the knee or hock.
STRAW A type of bedding.
STRIPE A narrow white mark down the front of the face.
SUFFOLK PUNCH A breed of heavy horse, always chestnut in colour.

T

TENNESSEE WALKING HORSE An American breed, noted for its running walk, which makes it comfortable to ride for long distances.
THOROUGHBRED The present-day English racehorse. Three Arabian sires started the breed, the Godolphin Arabian, the Darley Arabian, and the Byerley Turk.
TROT A pace of two beats.

W

WALL EYE One which has white or blue-white where the normal colour should be.
WEAVING A stable vice. The horse sways from side to side in his box, shifting his weight from one foot to the other. Usual cause—boredom.
WELSH COB A breed of cob deriving from the Welsh mountain pony.
WITHERS The part of the horse at the base of the neck.

ACKNOWLEDGMENTS

Acknowledgments are due to the following agencies for use of photographs:

W. W. Rouch & Co. Ltd. for "Tudor Minstrel" on half-title page.

Sport & General Press Agency Ltd. for the photograph on the title page; "Polo at Cowdray Park" p. 65; "Steeplechasing at Cheltenham" p. 66; "Col. C. B. R. Hornung's Stud" p. 67; "A Pony Club Rally" p. 68.

Foto Tidemann for "Mrs. V. D. S. Williams" p. 66.

Fox Photos for "Trekking in the Lorna Doone Valley" p. 69.

Peter A. Harding for "Lt.-Col. Frank Weldon" p. 69.

Monty, Birmingham 14, for photograph on p. 64.

Acknowledgment is also due to the Director of the British Museum for permission to reproduce "Horsemen in the Panathenaic Procession" p. 19, and to the Director of the Glasgow Art Gallery for permission to reproduce Joseph Crawhall's sketch of Tod Sloan p. 23.

My personal thanks to K.L.P. Film Services Ltd. for all the photographs in this book not otherwise acknowledged, and especially to Mr. C. A. Pockett not only for his professional skill in photographing the horses, but for all his patience and help.

The sketches on p. 60 illustrating hand signals are based on the pamphlet issued by the Royal Society for the Prevention of Accidents.

I would also like to say how grateful I am to my wife, our horses and ponies, our small staff and our many friends who ride with us. Without them this book would not have been possible. My special thanks to Mrs. Alice Timms for the encouragement she has given me in its preparation.

P.C.